Building a Mobile DJ Light S

By Jordar

Table of Contents

Preface

Why I wrote this Book

My first taste of the wedding and events world came when I was just 16 years old. I was attending a summer youth church camp, and the night we had anxiously awaited had arrived; the night of our dance party. I was accustomed to attending church dances and seeing a bored looking leader seated behind a folding table playing songs back to back from his iTunes playlist. This time, however, was different. Before me stood a young, hip-looking college student with some wondrous DJ toys before him. Intrigued, I spent most of the night standing beside his table, watching him masterfully mix track after track into one beautiful stream of music. The next week when I arrived home, I eagerly spent every bit of my small savings on a 2 CD Gemini all-in-one mixer. Right there in my bedroom, I taught myself to beat match and mix my favorite songs together, and my love of DJing was born. Around a year later, I decided it was time to start making money with my newfound talent. I managed to tell enough people I was a DJ that a cheerleader from my high school (who can convince any 16-year-old boy of anything) asked me to do the music for her sister's wedding for $50. Well, I was resolved to show up to this wedding with more than just a mixer and cheap PA system: I needed lights! I took to eBay and settled on my first DJ light ever; a simple sound-activated Chauvet Color Bank. 4 glorious bulbs that changed to the beat of the music, what more could I ask for! From the second I unpacked that basic light from its Styrofoam packaging, I was addicted.

A lot has changed since then. The Color Bank is long gone, and so are many other DJ lights I have used along the way. My addiction to lighting, fortunately, is as strong as ever. I sometimes wonder if my wife looks at the packages arriving every week to our doorstep and wonders if we are going bankrupt. Now, my closets are filled with the newest LED wash lights, moving heads, and other goodies that I am lucky enough to use weekly to help make people's events extraordinary.

Lighting is a powerful tool for the mobile DJs' arsenal. Once upon a time, people hired DJs solely based on their ability to find the best records and masterfully mix them at their event. With the advent of digital DJing, online music downloads, YouTube videos on how to become a DJ, and all of the other resources available, simply finding and playing music is no longer the only determining factor for many people when hiring a DJ. While I firmly believe that, above all, a DJs performance and music are the root and base of any mobile DJ business, it has almost become necessary to offer potential clients more than just a large music library. Lighting can become the thing that sets you apart, **but only if you use it right.** What do I mean by that? The cost of lighting has decreased dramatically over the years, and costs continue to come down as technology evolves. This means that lighting is easily available to many different types of DJ, both hobbyist and professional. Unfortunately, many hobbyists and low-end DJs, or those that are unsure about lighting, settle for a few lights from the local guitar center, plug them in, and call it good. **If you follow this trend, your business will not stand out.** I want to help you understand how to professionally use lighting to create ambiance, mood, emotion, and drama at your events. I want to help DJs everywhere set themselves apart from the competition and create events that will dazzle and amaze their clients.

I am in no way the grandmaster of lighting. There are DJs doing productions for thousands of people that I would love to learn at the feet of. But I do spend hours every day watching videos, reading books, and honing my lighting skills, and I have learned a lot from many different sources. I owe a lot of my lighting knowledge and inspiration to Brian S. Redd and Jeremy Brech, two of my favorite YouTube DJ gurus, and I must thank them for all they do for the mobile DJ community. My goal with this book is to help the new DJ out there (or even the experienced veteran who never has made it past sound-activated lighting) to build a lighting system that looks clean, professional, and makes an impact. You don't need to be the largest production company in your area to offer quality lighting services to your clients. So feel free to start in whatever section you feel applies to you most! I hope you enjoy learning about lighting as much as I do.

Chapter 1 – Where do I start?

The many different types of DJ lighting

Jump onto your favorite music retailer's website and click on the lighting category. Did you get thousands of results? Did every single one look different from the next? When you first decide to start adding lighting to your DJ business, you might do a google search for "Best DJ lights for beginners" or look at the thousands of YouTube video unboxings where different DJs open the boxes of their new gear and tell you about it. What's the problem with doing this? You will get so many different opinions! Every DJ (for better or worse) prefers certain lighting. These differences in opinion can be caused by geographical area, experience, how a DJ was trained, and any other number of factors. So how do you know what fixtures you should start your collection with? In this first chapter, I am going to explain the different types of DJ lights available, their uses, and how they can be used together.

Wash Lighting

I start with wash lighting for a reason; I believe that it forms the base of any successful light show. After all, the whole point of a light show is to LIGHT the dancefloor. This helps to avoid accidents (tripping and falling), potential inappropriate behavior (dirty dancing at schools), and other consequences at your events. It also allows you to turn off the harsh overhead fluorescent lighting found at 90% of venues and create an atmosphere that is conducive to dancing. Wash lights do exactly what their name suggests; they wash an area with light, which is usually colored. Wash lights can be par fixtures, bar fixtures, or other unique designs such as the Chauvet WashFX (my current wash fixture of choice for large events). Did a lot of those words just go over your head? Here are a few quick definitions:

Par Light (PAR CAN): A PAR light, which stands for *parabolic anodized reflector*, was traditionally a light found in theaters, productions, and concerts that contained a bright halogen bulb in a parabolic (curved) housing that projected a strong, concentrated beam of light. With the advent of current LED technology, the name is no longer indicative of the exact function of the light but is still the common industry name for lights that project a focused beam.

Bar Fixture: A bar-shaped light is exactly what the name implies; a wash light laid out in a linear fashion that normally spreads the light over a greater horizontal distance and reduced vertical distance. Some bar wash lights can be "pixel mapped," allowing control of the individual LED diodes that permits the user to create stunning effects.

A simple LED par light

Wash lighting can be cheap; a par fixture like the one above can be had for $69 or $79 dollars. The par light above uses small **RGB LEDs**; separate LED diodes for red, green, and blue that combine to form the thousands of other colors the light is capable of producing. Some par fixtures, such as the American DJ Mega TriPar Profile, combine the RGB diodes into something called **Tri LEDs**. By combining the colors together under a single lens, color mixing is improved and individual color "shadows" are drastically reduced.

Although red, green, and blue are the standard base colors found in all wash lighting, other diode colors can be added, such as specific white diodes, amber (yellow), and even ultraviolet (UV)! Wash lights with these added colors cost more but allow you to achieve more color mixing options such as hot pink and lime green which are unable to be accurately produced with RGB wash lighting. For a DJ starting out, RGB wash lighting will serve the majority of your needs.

TIP: If you mainly do weddings, you can benefit greatly from a par with white and amber diodes. One of the most popular colors at weddings is a warm white or amber, and these colors are achieved best with dedicated white and amber diodes.

A good place to start your lighting journey would be 2 or 4 LED wash. I always recommend buying wash lighting in pairs due to **symmetry**, which is something we will discuss further on. Do some research for a light that fits your needs and budget. Here are my recommendations for beginner par lighting, with prices I found on Amazon at the time of writing:

American DJ Mega Par Profile Plus - $79
A simple light from a reputable company that includes UV diodes for blacklight color mixing and effects. This par is cheap enough that you can buy 2 or 4 and obtain a nice wide area of coverage on your dance floor.

American DJ Mega Hex Par - $99
By stepping up $20 a light, you get a HEX LED par fixture! You are going to get better color mixing, brighter output, new color diodes that would be perfect for wedding DJs (and any DJ really).

American DJ 5P HEX Par - $179
This small light packs a punch, giving you a Hex LED (6 colors) par with greater output than the lights mentioned above for DJs that do larger events.
While there are many other wash lights you can choose from, these are a few options that are on the cheaper end of the scale. Do your research and look at lights from other companies such as Chauvet and Blizzard lighting. Compare the colors available and whether the diodes are separate or combined.

TIP: Be on the lookout for lighting packs that combine 4 or 8 fixtures with a bag and power cables! These packs usually allow you to get everything you need to start your light show at a reduced price and without having to order multiple items. A quick search for "par lighting pack" on your favorite gear supplier should get you headed in the right direction.

Effect Lighting

The next step in building your light show will most likely be effect lighting. Effect lighting brings more motion and energy to your light show. While there are many different types of effect lighting, the majority function by focusing light through lenses into beams that create patterns on the wall or dance floor. Effect lights can have motors inside that move the diodes in circles, back and forth, or other configurations. These lights are the ones that remind most people of a dance party or disco. Effect lights are great additions to your light show; they add lots of movement and cover large areas, giving you a lot of bang for your buck. While I don't suggest using them the whole event (more on that in a later chapter), they definitely add variety to a light show. A lot of DJs are tempted to start with effect lighting before they purchase wash lighting, but I strongly suggest you get yourself some quality wash lights before venturing into effect light territory (remember, **form a good base**). Some examples of effect lights that are great to start out with are:

Chauvet DJ Mini Kinta IRC - $89
The Kinta creates a wide coverage of LED light and is simple to operate. With how cheap this light is, I suggest getting a pair (remember, symmetry). This light works by projecting an array of beams across the room and moving them in an "over-under" pattern to the beat of the music.

American DJ Vertigo Hex - $99
This classic effect (the "mushroom") has been updated by ADJ with hex LEDs, giving you all of those awesome colors that aren't well produced by simple RGB LEDs. Like the Kinta, this light sprays a massive spread of beams across your room that rotate and dance to the beat of the music (as picked up by the unit's internal microphone).

An LED mushroom light with fog

Effect lighting is one of the most dynamic and interesting categories of lighting. Manufacturers are constantly innovating, changing, and updating their fixtures by adding more features each year. Beyond the simple, classic effects I mentioned above are dozens of designs that are completely unique.

TIP: The more specialized and unique a light is, the more limited the number of situations you can use said light in. While some effects are insanely cool to us, they may not be practical for the majority of our events. At the beginning, seek out lights that are universal and can be used in a variety of gig situations.

Moving Heads and Scanners

Now we are moving into the "big guns." Moving heads and scanners are often called intelligent lights because they can be controlled via DMX (more on DMX in a later chapter). In the case of **scanners**, they feature a mirror connected to a motor that reflects the beam of light all around the room. With a moving head, the entire fixture moves and aims the beam of light. Moving heads are the lights you see at concerts and festivals sweeping over the crowd and stage. Thanks to LED technology and great manufacturers, these lights have become affordable and easily available, whereas in the past they were mostly reserved for touring and larger production companies. They were bulky, heavy, and cumbersome. Today's moving heads and scanners have been optimized for the mobile DJs, with some examples fitting in a single hand! Moving heads and scanners really add to the professional image of your light show, because people associate their effects with larger productions.

Inside of a moving head or scanner are various wheels. The color wheel contains colored gels that change the color of the beam of light. The gobo wheel contains (you guessed it) gobos. **Gobos** act like stencils, changing the circular spotlight into patterns and shapes. Scanners for mobile DJs can be had as cheap as $199 and moving heads at only $299. Obviously, the more you spend, the brighter and more feature-packed fixture you will get. Here are a few good options to consider for your first light show:

American DJ Pocket Scan - $199
A pair of these lights is a great intelligent lighting addition to your show. They are powerful enough for small parties, extremely compact, and have great internal programs inside. They also come in a 2 light pack with a bag and cables.

American DJ Pocket Pro - $299

A great first moving head with various colors, gobos, and a decently bright LED (which was just updated from a 12 watt LED to a 25 watt LED). One great benefit of this moving head is its **Powercon** connector, which is a locking power plug that assures your light won't easily come unplugged.

Chauvet Intimidator Spot 155 - $399

My moving head of choice, these little guys have a 32watt LED (plenty bright for most mobile DJs), separate color and gobo wheels, and even split colors! This head also has a **power output** plug so that you can link multiple lights together without running separate power cords, a super handy feature that helps with a clean-looking truss.

A small LED moving head light

TIP: With the lower price of today's moving head fixtures, it might be worth considering skipping over effect lights and purchasing a pair of moving heads right away. While not essential for a quality light show, they certainly are rarer than effect lights and you will stand out more from your competition if they are used effectively.

Lasers, Strobe Lights, UV Lights, and Other Specialty Lights

Specialty lights can be some of the most fun! Unfortunately, they are the most *application specific*. Lasers can really wow event guests if used right. But using them at a wedding? There are probably better choices (the wedding photographer might hate you if you aim them at that beautiful white dress). Strobe lights can make the epic dubstep drop even more epic. They can also blind people and tick them off (epilepsy anyone?). They work great at high school dances and college parties, but not so much at a corporate event. The most important question to ask whenever you are about to purchase a light is "When will I use this?" and "Will I be able to make my money back using this light?" And maybe most important, "How versatile is this light?" This part of purchasing lights can be the hardest because if you are like me you want to buy as many cool lights as possible. Thinking back to my own experiences, I remember over the past few years spending hours poring over lighting websites and magazines and buying whatever light was the newest and most unique. If a light went on sale I snatched it up, all the while justifying how I would incorporate it into my show. I was convinced that I would someday be designing light shows for huge concerts and auditoriums and that, of course, I would be able to make that fixture feel right at home! The problem; that isn't the direction my company took. While I was hoping I would be spending the majority of my weekends DJing for proms, college dances, and frat parties, I've ended up deeply planted inside the wedding market. Now, 80% of my lighting spends its weekends inside its bags and cases in my garage. Do I still enjoy the rare occasions I get to take those lights out, fill a venue with haze, and fill the space with beams, strobes, and lasers? Of course! But am I getting a significant ROI on my purchases? Not at all.

So as you begin your lighting journey, especially if the whole DJ business is a new avenue for you, evaluate each lighting purchase and how versatile it will be for you. As you grow and expand and discover your niche in the market, *then* you can decide which specialty lighting will serve you best.

A small galaxian-style DJ laser

Bonus: All-in-one Systems

One of the best innovations I have seen in compact mobile DJ lighting over the past few years has been the all-in-one systems offered by both Chauvet DJ and American DJ. Take, for example, the Chauvet GigBar LT (my lighting rig of choice for small, simple weddings). For under $300, you not only get 3 separate lighting effects but a great case, a tripod stand, cables, a foot switch, and a wireless remote! To me, this eliminates the biggest hassle associated with lighting at smaller events; spending the majority of my setup time hanging lights, connecting cables, and wrapping them to look professional. With a GigBar or similar system, the hassle of cable management is eliminated and you can have a light show set up in less than 2 minutes. Talk about a great way to get your foot in the door with lighting! The system comes with 2 wash pars, 2 moonflower effect lights, and 4 strobes across the top that do eye-catching chases.

Other great options in the category are the full sized Chauvet GigBar and the American DJ Dotz TPar system. If you already own a T-bar or other lighting stand, both American DJ and Chauvet make some amazing multi-effect lights that give you a huge bang for your buck. For example, the Swarm 4 FX from Chauvet offers dual moonflowers, a strobe ring, and a laser in one convenient package. American DJ sells the popular Stinger series (and now the Startec series), which both contain multiple effects. These multi-effect lights can make for a dynamic show that is ultra-portable and easy on the wallet.

A Word on Chinese Off-Brand Lights

A lot of things are made in China. A lot. This includes most DJ lights. It's a fact we face in the modern world; it's simply cheaper (to everyone) to manufacture in China. So if you look at the bottom of your light fixtures and they say "MADE IN CHINA," don't be alarmed. But there is one trend you need to watch out for, and that is purchasing lighting from eBay or Amazon that is not from a trusted manufacturer and comes directly from China. Many Chinese companies are offering lighting that looks very similar to the models offered by Chauvet, American DJ, Blizzard, and the like. They have the same shape, same claimed power rating, same DMX channels, etc.… But are they the same? NO. I can speak to you from cold hard experience that these lights are NOT the same as those offered by major lighting companies.

While they may look the same, the materials are poor, the workmanship is subpar, and the quality control is nonexistent. I made the mistake of ordering 4 knock-offs that were extremely similar looking to the Blizzard Flurry Wash. The Blizzards are $399 a piece; the Chinese ones, $99 each. What a steal, right? WRONG. While they looked similar to their Blizzard counterparts, their cheap plastic exteriors became separated almost as soon as they were taken out of the box. Panning and tilting was a glitchy nightmare, with jittery movements the norm. Randomly, a light would enter auto mode and begin to rotate and strobe without reason. And let's not forget the manual, which appeared to be written by a 10-year-old foreign exchange student. If one of these lights went out, I was straight out of luck. The majority of these companies offer no customer support.

Long story short: don't cheap out on your lighting. Buying lights from trusted companies offers peace of mind that far outweighs the difference in cost. Most lights are made from extremely durable plastics or metals and come with both support and a warranty. You will spend much more, in the long run, replacing broken fixtures when you choose to buy off-brand. Save your money, and buy quality.

Chapter 2 – The Lighting Nitty Gritty

The technical side of things

I'm no electrician. I'd probably electrocute myself if I tried to fix anything electrical in my house. But the good news for you and me is that you don't need to be an electrician to get a jump on other DJ companies in DJ lighting. There are a few little specs you can look at when purchasing lights and planning your rig that will help you get the most return on investment and avoid electrical problems at your events.

Watts

Watts are an indication of how much power your lights are using. Back before LED lighting, lamps found inside DJ lights pulled huge amounts of power. It wasn't uncommon for an effect light to use 300 watts of power, which is not something to bat an eye at! Luckily, nowadays LED lights are extremely efficient. Some effect lights only use 10-15 watts, and are still very bright! We are going to go over brightness in the next section of this chapter, but the most important part of the watt rating of a fixture is to know how many lights you can daisy chain together. By daisy chaining lights together, you can run a power cord from one light to the next, without having run a power cable from each light to an outlet. Look on the manufacturer's website or in the light manual for the number of fixtures you can hook together, but be aware this rating is only for identical fixtures.

Lumens & Lux

These specs are more indicative of a light's brightness. Whenever I am trying to pick a light fixture based on brightness, I always look at the LUX value. *Watts mean squat if the LED is not using those watts efficiently.* For example, I was looking to buy new scanners or moving heads. The reason I decided to use the Chauvet Intimidator Spot 155 is that its seemingly small 32 watt LED boasts almost 5,000 LUX at 2 meters; much more than other LED moving heads near that price point!

A word about LEDs vs. discharge lamps

For 95% of your needs, LED lighting is the way to go. It's more power efficient, runs cooler, and offers vivid colors. Not to say that there is not a place for traditional bulbs! If you make your way to providing lighting for large events, upper range moving heads make use of powerful discharge lamps that offer extremely high LUX values. However, for those that do weddings, birthday parties, and small dances LED lighting is the way to go. It's lightweight, safe, and practical. Form your lighting rig around LED lighting.

TIP: Don't fall into the trap of purchasing ancient, used lighting from craigslist and other stores! These lights are usually either broken, ugly, or extremely power hungry. If it looks like it was made in the 80s, you're better off buying new. Always look at your lighting purchases from the client's point of view and think "Would I want this at my event?"

Power Linking

A great feature to have in your lighting is the ability to power link. This feature is practically standard on any fixture made by the big names in lighting. Power linking allows multiple fixtures to be daisy chained together in order to avoid too many cables from cluttering your setup. American DJs version of power linking features IEC output (IEC connections are common in technology and computing). Chauvet, on the other hand, uses normal AC Edison plug outlets on their lights. This is why I'm partial to Chauvet lights; I don't need to purchase separate cables to link my fixtures. Both versions, however, function well and eliminate clutter from your setup.

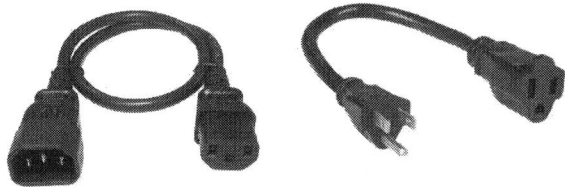

An IEC extension vs a normal AC extension cord

Clamps

Once you have your lighting, you're going to need a way to hang it. There are many different styles of lighting clamps, but the most common is the O-clamp. An O clamp (not surprisingly) looks like an O. This circular clamp is fitted with a bolt that swivels closed and tightens down to keep your lighting snugly on your stand of choice. Plastic O-clamps are durable and can support a decent amount of weight and work great on T-bars and basic I-beam trussing. Another model of clamp is the **trigger clamp.** These work by hooking over your truss (instead of wrapping around) and clamping on. They are quick and painless and can cut your rigging time significantly. Most manufacturers also offer slim versions of their clamps, which reduce form factor and blend in better. If you are using metal trussing to support your lights, stronger metal clamps are available. Some clamps can support hundreds of pounds of weight! Not that you'll need that for your first lighting rig, but it's fun to think about.

Chapter 3 – Getting Your Lights Off the Ground

Because lighting the guests' pants isn't too effective

If you want to get me really riled up, take me to an event where the DJ has his lights set on the ground. Or his table. Or a chair. Or basically anywhere someone would set their drink or drunken girlfriend. Lighting on the ground is my biggest pet peeve. Why? Because that practically destroys the purpose of lighting. Light doesn't travel through solid objects. Setting lighting on the floor will assure that those closest to the DJ booth are blind, and those in the back are stumbling over each other. Even if you only have 2 LED PARs to your name and nothing more, getting those PARs properly mounted above the dance floor will do wonders for your setup. Setting light fixtures on the ground is detrimental to your company image. Nothing could say "I'm lazy" more than being too cheap to buy a $7.00 clamp and lift the light off of the ground. Did that hurt someone's feelings? I'm sure it did. But it's a fact of life. I'm sure I will get someone who will say "But Jordan! What about if I am on a stage?" or "Jordan, you're being ridiculous. I think the effect of aiming lights at the ceiling is neat!" But my opinion, which has come from looking at dozens and dozens of DJs setups, is that the DJs who are making money doing high-end events, the ones who get clients who understand their worth, know that the majority of lighting belongs on a stand. In the next few sections, I'm going to go over the various types of DJ lighting stands, their uses, and when each works best.

Speaker Stands

If your budget is completely gone, and you're not sure how you are going to get your lights off the ground, mounting a light to each speaker tripod is a great option, albeit with a few drawbacks. Your lights will be able to cover more area when they are suspended a few feet above the floor, even if they are below your speakers. On the flipside, lights mounted below speakers sit right about eye level, which could mean your hardest partiers could be seeing stars most of the night. Mounting lighting below speakers can actually work really well in some situations; I have seen a few DJs mount *Inno Pocket Spot Duos* (dual moving head fixtures from American DJ) to the underside of their speakers with great success. Some DJ speakers come with fly points on the top, which are threaded holes used to "fly" the speaker overhead, and I have seen some DJs successfully mount trussing or a T-Bar to the top of their speaker for lighting (slightly tacky in some situations). When it comes down to it, I recommend you splurge and buy a dedicated lighting stand or truss like the ones below.

T-Bars

Ah, the humble T-bar. My first lighting stand was probably what many of your first lighting stands will be; a 9 or 10-foot tripod stand fitted with a 3-foot bar across the top. Is it sexy? Not quite. Does it get your lighting where it needs to be? Absolutely. A T-bar stand can be obtained cheaply: as low as $50 or $60. They extend to a great height, can hold a few lights, and look even better in pairs.

For maybe the first 2 years I owned my little DJ company, I mounted 2 wash lights and a centerpiece on my trusty T-bar and I felt like the coolest cat on the block. Some of the pros of the T-bar include quick setup, low cost, small footprint, easy to pack, and lightweight. Some of the cons are not enough room for more fixtures, being a potential eyesore (especially when only using 1), and being basic (most DJs use them). When you're faced with the choice of lights on the floor or using a T-bar, always opt for the T-bar.

I-Beam Trussing

After your lighting setup has grown, a logical next step could be an I-beam truss setup such as the American DJ LTS-50 ($199). This 10-foot-long span of metal trussing is black and blends in well at events. It can hold quite a few more fixtures than a T-bar and looks better while doing it. While this definitely isn't a system I would bring to most weddings, it looks great at sweet 16s, grad parties, college events, and other similar get-togethers. I owned my LTS-50 for around a year and had some great events with large light shows. As an example, I mounted 2 led strip lights down the vertical posts, 4 moving heads underneath, 2 LED black light strips across the top, and an effect light in the center. It was a high impact show that the kids loved. The pros of the I-beam truss are greater weight capacity, increased light capacity, sturdier, and a larger overall impact. The cons are more space needed to haul it, harder to hide at classier events, and the feeling that it's not quite a large setup, but not a small one either. The best part about the I-beam system is that when you do need to scale down for small events, you can simply use one of the included tripod stands and an included T-bar to make a smaller lighting setup.

Truss

Up until the past few years, professional grade trussing was only available to concert level touring acts and DJs with extremely deep pockets. Luckily, the price of trussing and the ease of obtaining it has made it a viable option for even part-time mobile DJs. The most common form of trussing used in the entertainment industry is the 12" diameter box truss. Companies such as Global Truss America manufacture lengths of this truss from 1 foot to 14 feet and more. It's extremely strong and capable of supporting hundreds and even thousands of pounds of gear. It's shiny metallic finish really gives a grand impression to those who see it. However, the benefits of professional trussing come at a price; a 6-foot section of box truss will set you back around $250, and that's not including base plates, connectors, and junctions. I won't go into the details of trussing in this book, but when you come to the point where you would like to move to using trussing, there are many resources available online to help you in your decisions.

TIP: Getting into trussing is an easy way to set yourself apart from budget DJs, as the initial investment keeps many a hobbyist away. A high impact wedding setup could consist of two 6.5 foot truss totems (one on each side of your booth) with a moving head on top and a wash light attached to the side. This type of setup can be observed on many a pro DJs Facebook page and really does look both high-end and professional.

All-in-one Systems

Just like with lighting, different companies offer package deals and pre-made systems that can ease the stress of determining what size of truss you need, what connections, etc.… The American DJ Light Bridge system is a great entry-level kit that consists of 2 extremely heavy duty crank up stands, along with 10 feet of miniature triangular trussing (still capable of holding 300 lbs.). Or you could consider a prepackaged truss totem system, consisting of 2 lengths of box trussing, bottom base plates, and top base plates. Totems are a popular choice among wedding DJs and offer a sleek, sophisticated look to brides and grooms. Lastly, you might consider the even cheaper glo-totems which are made from lengths of single tubes attached to base plates and wrapped in fabric called a scrim. By placing a par light (remember what that is?) inside these glo-totems, you have a lighting effect in and of itself. If you feel like stepping up into a full truss arch or goal post setup, both Chauvet and Global Truss offer triangular truss packages that consist of truss sections, connectors, pins, and base plates. I'm partial to the Global Truss Arch System, as it can be easily expanded by purchasing additional lengths of truss and connectors.

No matter how you choose to rig your lighting, even rigging it at all puts you leaps and bounds above many DJs. Whether you go the route of the simple T-Bar or step right up to the trussing you will be adding the professional polish to your light show that it needs to stand out.

Chapter 4 – Making it Look Pretty

Your image is vital to a client's perception of your skill

So by now, you should have a good idea of the many types of DJ lighting fixtures, how they function, and how to get them in the air so people can see them. Congrats! Chapter 4 is where I hopefully start to help you separate yourself from the hordes of other DJs who flood craigslist, undercutting you and stealing your business. Why are craigslist DJs able to steal clients from you in the first place? Aren't you different? More professional and experienced? While you may possess the skills and attention to detail that hobbyist DJs do not, **if your setup looks the same as theirs, clients will think of you as similar.** So learning to set up your lighting (and your other equipment) in a professional, clean, and sleek way is vital to the growth of your DJ business. The greatest thing about chapter 4 is that you don't need to spend loads of money to implement these tips. In fact, you don't really need to spend much at all. Mostly, this chapter is about learning to care enough about your company to show up 5 minutes earlier and dedicate that time to polishing the look of your setup so that clients know you mean business. So with that, let's jump into one of my favorite chapters.

Cable Management

Remember how I said lighting on the floor was my biggest pet peeve? Poor cable management is a close second. Proper cable management requires no money (except maybe a roll of Velcro straps from the Wal-Mart electrical section, a whopping $3.50) and only a small time investment. Below is a picture of what I consider terrible cable management.

That makes me cringe. Ok, ok, that's an extreme example. Let me put up another picture.

Not as drastic this time, and honestly, we've all seen way too many DJ setups similar to this one. Does this look like yours? You might want to consider reading the tips that follow. Now before you get offended and leave a negative review of my book, let's look at one more picture.

Now obviously, we have jumped up a few levels here. But how do you think this mobile DJ got to this point? Do you think if he provided a setup like the first, he would get hired by the types of clients willing to pay money for a setup this size? Absolutely not. Take a look at that picture. Not a wire in site. Nothing to distract from the pure beauty that is his setup. If you want to attract clients who will pay you the kind of money to afford totems and moving heads like that, you need to play the part. And the first step is proper cable management.

There really isn't much to it. Take a trip to your local Walmart and purchase a pack of Velcro straps. You can get a roll of gray and black ones for about $3.50. Now set up your equipment in your room for a test run. Are wires hanging down from your lighting stand? Run those wires across the top T-bar and use a Velcro strap or two to keep them snugly behind and out of view. As you run the wires down your vertical support, use a Velcro strap at the top and bottom to keep them out of sight and out of mind. Was that so hard? If you're using triangle or box truss, it's even easier. Run your wires inside of your truss and Velcro them like you would on a T-bar. Make sure to run power cords away from audio cables, and if they must cross, make sure they do so as infrequently as possible and always at right angles.

Scrim

Whenever I think of scrim, I think of a leotard. Kind of a weird mental connection, but it works for me. Scrim is a stretchable fabric that is connected to the legs and vertical post of speaker or lighting stands to, you guessed it, hide wiring. Personally, I am more a fan of properly hiding wires with Velcro than using a scrim, but many DJs find scrim an easy and professional solution for hiding wires. Good scrim isn't cheap; a single speaker stand scrim from Scrim King (the biggest name in the business) can set you back $100, but if that look fits into your business plan, it can be a great investment. If you are using box truss, a scrim "sock" that slides over the length of your trussing and is lit from inside is an eye-catching, clean look with minimal effort.

TIP: My favorite application of scrim is to my DJ table itself, where I feel it looks 100 times more professional than a standard tablecloth. The tight, unwrinkled fabric lends an air of professionalism to the booth that a draped tablecloth may not.

Symmetry

Whenever I speak with local DJs, either individually or at meetings, I always bring up **symmetry**. To me, it's one of the easiest ways to make a mobile DJ setup more pleasing to the eye. Humans naturally find comfort in symmetry, and asymmetrical DJ setups can be a huge distraction to guests. On the next page are examples of both an asymmetrical DJ setup on the left, and a symmetrical DJ setup on the right.

Asymmetrical vs symmetrical DJ setups

Which setup is more pleasing to the eye? The left picture is not a bad setup: great wire management, a good façade, and overall a clean look. But your eyes, instead of focusing on the setup as a whole, or on the DJ in the middle, are drawn to the single subwoofer on the left, then back to the light tripod on the right, and back and forth until you grow bored of looking at it. Suppose the subwoofer was placed in the middle and the lighting tripod in the back center of the setup. Now your eyes would be drawn to the center focal point. Now, look at the setup on the right. Once again, a quality setup with great cable management, simple but strong lighting, and my favorite part, symmetry. Each side has the same amount of speakers, subs, and lighting tripods. Naturally, your eyes take the setup in as a while and focus on the center point, where a DJ would be standing.

It's simple, isn't it? Now obviously different circumstances will dictate whether you can implement this strategy at every event. I have had my fair share of events where clients have shoved my setup and I into a small space with no room behind me for a lighting tripod. But, in the vast majority of cases, you can make this method work with minimal effort. Something I did not quite understand when I first started out was to buy lights in pairs. Buying lighting in sets of 2 or 4 helps to keep your setup symmetrical. I used to own 3 different DJ effect lights and a big wash panel, and I would throw those suckers on a T-bar, Velcro my wires, and call it good (you can see the picture below, on the left). The problem was, each light was shaped differently and produced a different effect. The effect on my dance floor was a chaotic mess of colors and shapes that mostly upset the stomachs of guests instead of pumping them up. Whenever possible, aim to buy lights in pairs. Wash lighting should always be bought in pairs, as well as scanners and moving heads. A single, bright effect light can serve as a centerpiece, but if it is going to be placed to the right or the left of center make sure you have a second fixture to complement it.

One of my early setups (asymmetrical) vs a newer (symmetrical) setup

Keeping it Simple

This tip is sometimes the hardest for people to grasp. When my gear addiction first started, and I was obsessed with having every new light on the market in my setup, I would wind up bringing lighting to events that A) the client did not pay for, or B) weren't necessary for the particular event I was at. Don't fall into this trap! Listen, I know these "toys" we get to play with are fun; ask my wife, she deals with it daily. But when it all comes down to it, bringing every light you own to every gig just clutters up your image. At a small wedding do I really need 3 effect lights, 4 wash bars, a laser, and a mirror ball? Maybe if the client paid me for that specifically, but more often than not, a small intimate wedding can benefit greatly from 2 simple wash lights for the dance floor and one underneath a white tablecloth or 2 against the wall behind you.

One of the most common and best-looking wedding lighting systems is a totem on each side of the booth, with an LED par inside, an LED par under your white tablecloth to make it glow, and a par or two against the wall behind the DJ. While there is no effect lighting involved in this setup, the glow emanating from the DJ area (during the dancing portion of the night) usually radiates out onto the dancefloor and creates a great effect. If you want to go a little more intricate, maybe for a larger wedding or a sweet 16, you could do a T-bar on each side of your setup with 2 wash lights (one per end of the T-bar) and a center effect light on each T-bar. By angling these T-bars slightly inward toward the dance floor, you can focus the energy on the guests and away from the surrounding tables and chairs. The point of all of this? **Sometimes being a minimalist isn't such a bad idea.**

It might go against everything you believe in and everything your DJ instincts do not want you to do. It might bum you out because you have fixtures sitting at home while you are out gigging (although if you did your research and bought the correct lights this is less of a problem). But in the eyes of those that see your setups, a simple and effective light show will have much more impact than a large and cluttered light show.

TIP: There are a lot of clichés and stigmas that follow DJs around. "Cheesy" is a common one, but "cluttered" is one I hear often as well. Too many people are used to seeing a DJ as the guy (or gal) that shows up with a truckload of bulky gear that they haphazardly throw in a corner. Be different! There are plenty of DJs showing up with 25 lights at events and making guests nauseous; be the DJ who shows up with the perfect number of lights to create just the right atmosphere without lacking or being overbearing.

Chapter 5 – Lighting Design

Creating setups that don't all look the same

One of the most important things I want you to understand from this book is **that you don't need to have an enormous light show to impress your clients.** I used to think that I needed to have every type of light on the market and I needed to use them all of the time if I wanted to stay competitive. That's not the case! I may sound like a hypocrite because of all the lighting I buy now, but trust me, you don't need to spend thousands to have a quality light show. The key to a good light show is **variety.** It's about doing things different than other DJs. You have to be unique if you want people to see a value in your service. Now, this doesn't mean go crazy and start shoving pars into random corners and on top of shelves and stands willy-nilly. What you need is a **plan.** One of my favorite activities on my day off is setting up my light show in my living room (I'm a nerd, I know). That way, I can experiment with different light placement, colors, angles, and other aspects I simply don't have time for when setting up for a gig. In the following sections, you will find a few different aspects of your lighting you can vary to create interesting looks.

Depth

Adding lighting depth means that all of your lights aren't arranged in a single file line all of the time. Sure, this is necessary and desired for some events, but most of the time, you can change the location of different lights to add depth to your light show. What do I mean exactly? Take your wash lighting for example. Let's image you have 4 LED par lights. You could line all 4 up along the top of your T-bar and your light show will look good. **It will also look like most DJs' light setup.** Now let's say you leave 2 pars on the T-bar to flood your dance floor, and you move 2 pars behind your setup, against the wall pointing up to create **uplights** (more on uplights later, but for now know that uplighting is placing lights on the ground against the wall to create columns of light). Boom! You have created depth, and your light show is *different*. What if you left 2 pars on the T-bar, and put the other 2 on your speaker stands? Or mounted them on top of your speakers? Some speakers have rigging points on top that allow lights to be mounted on them. See how easy it was to add depth with just 4 par lights? You can do this with any lighting setup. If you are using I-beam truss, add lighting to the vertical posts, and mount some lights both above and below the truss. If you are using LED bars, position them diagonally instead of horizontally. There are limitless options.

Color

Using different colors in your lighting is a great way to add depth. Because we haven't talked about lighting control or DMX yet, a great way to run your wash lighting is on static color mode (especially during slow moments at weddings). By using separate colors for the lighting on your truss and the lighting on the ground or speakers, you can create depth. Take a moment to search the internet for information about colors that work well together. If you're too lazy for that, here is a primer: Red, yellow, and orange are strong colors that evoke emotions like happiness, anger, and energy. Blues, greens, and purples are calmer colors. Pinks and whites are very laid back and preferred by (you guessed it) a lot of brides. Put together colors in the same family (such as red and pink or purple and blue) or those that are opposite on the color wheel (my personal favorite combination is yellow and blue). I love to use two colors, as it adds a lot to a light show. I usually avoid more than 3 colors at once and primarily stick to 2 at a time.

TIP: Show the client you really understand their event's vision by matching your lighting to the situation. Doing an "under the sea" themed school dance? Fill the dance with blue and aqua colored lighting. How about a rustic, candle-filled mountain wedding? Dim amber uplights would be magical.

Creating Contrast

After you have been purchasing and offering lighting for a while, you will probably have a few different lights of different types. Hopefully, you've started with some wash lighting, gotten some effect lighting, and maybe even purchased some scanners or moving heads. If you were to show up to a gig and just turn all of your lights on at once and leave them, you would have a multi-colored mess that would be far from visually pleasing. **This is the route most mobile DJs take.** You are not like most mobile DJs! Leaving every fixture you brought with you on automatic mode the entire dance is BORING. You will wear out your guests' eyes and interest quickly. Having the restraint to only turn certain lights on at certain moments will do wonders for your light show. In the next chapter on DMX, we will go over how to turn lights on and off through programming, but you don't even need to get that complicated to take control of your light show. American DJ just came out with the Airstream Wi-Fi Pack ($99), which is a viable option for simple lighting control.

American DJ Airstream Wi-Fi Pack

This 8-outlet power strip is Wi-Fi controllable, meaning you can turn the power to your light fixtures on and off with an iPad app! How cool is that? Other companies make power strips that can be turned on and off remotely with switches and remotes. Regardless of how you control your lighting, the most important part is knowing when to use each effect. Wash lighting is good for almost any moment and is the only type of light I will leave on almost continually. Your effect lighting is higher energy, and turning them on for the most exciting parts of your set will amp the energy up. As an example, let's say you are using 2 LED bars for your wash lighting, 2 moonflower effect lights, and a pair of scanners. You could start the dance with your wash lighting and moonflower lights on. After a few songs, turn off the moonflowers and turn on your scanners. When you throw on an epic dance mix, turn off the wash lighting and use only the moonflowers and scanners. See how we are creating different looks with the same fixtures? This returns us to where we started: **variety.**

Only use what you need

Yep, we are back here again. Why? Because after giving you all of these ideas, I'm sure you're eager to go build the biggest baddest light show in town. But remember, **fit your rig to the event.** When I do a school homecoming, you can bet I will pull out almost every single light I own to make sure those kids feel like they are at a concert. But if I'm DJing a small 50 person wedding on a Thursday night with a shy bride and groom, a small all-in-one system is all I need (unless I have upsold additional lighting to the client).

Chapter 6 – DMX Control

The chapter you have all been waiting for

For many DJs, DMX is the great unknown. It's seen as the insurmountable wall of technical impediment that takes a rocket scientist to understand. In reality, DMX lighting control is not hard at all, it just takes a little time to understand. Just like riding a bike, once you understand the fundamentals you will be able to jump on any number of DMX controllers and use them to control lighting. In this chapter, I'm going to explain what DMX control is, your different options for controllers (hardware vs. software), and how to hook up your lights. I also plan to give a few simple ideas for programming, such as when to use fast programs and slow programs, movements and colors, and midi control. While you will hopefully be able to understand DMX by the end of this chapter, this is not a comprehensive guide. DMX is so much bigger than a few pages in a book, and I invite you to explore other videos and guides after reading this chapter to deepen your understanding of the particular capabilities of your controller and your lights.

TIP: After publishing this book and receiving a lot of feedback, I have published a second book titled "DMX For Mobile DJs: The Essential Guide." It goes into the origins of DMX and how to use it with much more depth than this book does and contains many step-by-step programming walkthroughs.

What is DMX?

Before DMX control, lighting was analog. Basically, you had the option to turn a certain light on or off and to dim it. That was it! As you can probably figure out, this meant light shows were much more basic than today's modern displays. With the invention of DMX, it opened the door to intelligent lighting, scanners, moving heads, and more. Now, instead of a simple on and off control, a light's position, beam angle, rotation, color, and more could be controlled remotely. DMX stands for "Digital Multiplex," and is often followed by the number 512. The number 512 represents the number of channels in one DMX "universe" (more on universes later). Each of those channels can control one attribute of a lighting fixture. For example, a channel can control the speed of a light's horizontal movement, it's brightness, or it's color. On DMX controllers, channels are almost always controlled by faders. These faders can be slid between values of 0 (off, or deactivated) to 255 (fully on). Cheaper DMX controllers can control as little as 3 or 4 channels (for a simple RGB PAR can) up to 512 channels and more. By running a cable from your controller to the *DMX INPUT* of a light, and then from the *DMX OUTPUT* of that light to the *DMX INPUT* of the next light and so on, you can link all of your lights together in one "daisy chain."

Does this sound like Chinese? Let me use a quick example: imagine you have an RGB par light. Imagine this light can be controlled with 4 channels, a so-called "4 channel fixture." The first channel controls the main dimmer, the second controls the amount of the color red, the third controls the amount of the color green, and the fourth controls the amount of the color blue. Suppose you brought the first dimmer up to the top (fully on) and then slowly brought up the red fader. You would see the red diodes in your fixture slowly fade from off to full brightness. Then, if you slowly brought up the blue fader, you would see your blue diodes fade in and combine with the red to form purple. In a simplified manner, that is how DMX works! Obviously, as we add more complicated fixtures and the number of channels within each light increases, we are met with virtually unlimited options. Within your light fixtures themselves, you can set the light to a specific *DMX address*, a number from 1 – 512. This helps each individual fixture to receive its *own instructions* from the DMX controller. If fixtures didn't have addresses, all of your lights would react simultaneously when you made adjustments to your controller, and it would be chaos!

DMX addressing allows you to control each light individually so you can create really amazing effects! As always, I believe examples help you to understand best, so here's an example: let's imagine the first light in your DMX chain is an LED par (it's the simplest light, so I use it in most examples). On the fixture's LED screen (or dipswitches if it is an older light) we would navigate to the DMX screen and set it to channel 001. While this screen will most likely be different on each fixture you own (consult the manual for your light for instructions on how to get to the DMX menu), most lights display "d001" on their DMX menu. Congrats! Now your first fixture is programmed to channel one. If you light has 4 channels of control, it will occupy channels 001 through 004.

Most lighting fixtures have the ability to change **channel modes.** Different channel modes determine exactly how many specific parameters of your light (such as dimmer, strobe, and colors) you will control with your DMX controller. For example, when controlling large amounts of lights via DMX, using 7, 10, or more channels per fixture will eat up your available channels fast. By putting your lights in lower channel mode (such as 4 or 5 channels), you will be able to control more lights. Sometimes, you don't need to get so intricate with your programming as to need 20 or 30 channels. For most beginners, being able to control 5 channels (dimmer, red diode, green diode, blue diode, and strobe) is plenty. *Be sure to look at your manuals and see which mode will give you access to the parameters you're looking to control.*

TIP: There are a lot of tradeoffs to be made while programming. Choosing a higher channel mode will allow you the greatest customization of your light, but usually is more time-intensive and, like I stated above, will eat up your available channels. When first starting out in DMX, one of the simpler channel modes is usually more than enough to create quality light shows.

By using the faders to adjust the attributes of your lights, you are able to create *scenes*. **A light scene is basically a snapshot of your lights when they are programmed a certain way that can be recalled at a later time.** For example, imagine you set your LED par lights to blue and set your effect lighting to red with a clockwise spin. Once you have all of your faders set how you like them and the lights look right, you store those settings as a *scene*. Then, during your event, you can press a button and recall those settings instantly to match a certain song or mood. By combining multiples scenes together, you can create *chases*, which are (you guessed it) sequences of scenes. For example, you could set all of your lights to red and save it as a scene. Then, you could program them all to blue and save that scene. Once more, you could program them to white and save that scene. Then, you could save those 3 scenes into a *chase*. At your event, you could recall that chase and the colors red, blue, and white would cycle through automatically.

TIP: Still confused? Read the last couple of paragraphs again, slowly and out loud (perhaps while following along with a DMX controller if you have one). I've found this to be the best way to digest complex instructions, and it is how I learned DMX. Sound hard? Don't worry, we'll practice it.

Which controller is best for me, hardware or software?

Up until the last few years, the majority of DJs used hardware controllers, such as the one pictured below. These standalone controllers are simple to use, portable, and able to produce great light shows.

A basic hardware DMX controller

On the left of the controller are buttons representing each of your fixtures. By selecting a button, the controller is now sending a signal to that light and you will see it react to your programming. This prevents all of your lights going crazy at the same time as you program each one. To the right of the fixture buttons are the faders. These control the individual channels of your lights. By sliding each fader up, you are moving that channel's value from 0% to 100%. The controller pictured allows 16 channels per fixture, meaning you can control light fixtures that have up to 16 channel attributes. But you may say, "Why are there only 8 faders if I can control 16 channels?" Great question. If you look closely to the right of the fader on the farthest right (don't include the set of 2 faders beneath the LED screen, those have another purpose), you will see a small button. This shift button changes the control of the faders from channels 1-8 of a fixture to 9-16. Now you can control the other half of your fixture's DMX attributes! However, you won't have to visit this second page of faders for a lot of fixtures. Many simple DJ lights only use 3, 4, 6, or 8 channels. However, if your fixture has more channels that you would like to use, that shift button allows you to reach them.

Above the faders, you will see 8 buttons. These are your scene buttons. When you program a light scene you like, you can save it to one of these scene buttons. But don't worry, you can program more than 8 scenes. To the right of that small LED screen at the top of the controller are 2 more buttons with up and down arrows printed next to them. These buttons allow you to change *scene pages.* So if you fill up the 8 scene buttons with awesome lighting scenes, simple click down to page 2 and program 8 more scenes! Most controllers allow you to store dozens, even hundreds of pages worth of lighting scenes. You probably won't run out!

As we move to the right side of the controller, we get to some more specialized buttons and faders. The 2 faders directly below the LED screen control the speed of your chases and the fade time of your scenes (how quickly they transition from one to another). The LED screen shows you what mode your controller is in, what scene and page number you are on, and more. The other buttons are used for programming (entering programming mode, saving scenes, etc.), blacking out the lights, turning on sound active mode, and other specialized functions. Because each controller is different, you'll want to thoroughly read your user's manual to understand your specific controller.

A software-based DMX controller works just like a hardware DMX controller, but on your computer's screen. Looking at a lighting control program, you will see faders and buttons just like you would on a hardware controller. A USB cable connects your computer to a small dongle or box that converts the USB signal into a DMX signal that can be sent to your lights. A great beginner DMX program and dongle is the **American DJ MYDMX Buddy ($99)**.

This small USB to DMX converter is super powerful and easy to program, cutting programming time to a fraction of what it is with a hardware DMX controller. With software, you can select your lights with simple drag and drop motions and select pre-programmed colors, chases, and even movements! Creating complex patterns and scenes for beginners is *much simpler* on a computer than a hardware controller. A great comparison of a hardware controller to a software controller would be using the command line to program lighting vs. using your desktop GUI. If you have an extra computer to spare, I would recommend you start with a software DMX controller vs a hardware controller. If you use a particularly powerful computer for DJing, it can probably run both your DJ software and lighting program simultaneously. There are pros and cons to each, but on the whole, a computer-based program will have a much easier learning curve for a beginner. However, be aware that computers aren't perfect and are more prone to malfunctions than a hardware controller, although this is true of your DJ mixer and other laptops as well.

DMX Cable and Terminators

Once you have a controller, you will need cabling to connect your lights. DMX cable comes in both 3 pin and 5 pin: for our purposes, we are only going to address 3 pin cabling. 3 pin DMX connections are the most common on fixtures aimed at the mobile DJ market and are what you will find on almost all of your lights. 5 pin DMX cable is largely used on professional lights out of the price range of the typical mobile DJ, although it is sometimes found adjacent to the 3 pin connectors.

Looking at a DMX cable, you will notice it bears a striking resemblance to the XLR cable you use for your microphones and speakers. There has been an online debate raging in forums for years about whether XLR microphone cable can be used as DMX cable (after all, they have the same connectors right?). There are many DJs who use cheap microphone cables to connect their lighting and who swear they have no issues. Those who have an understanding of the science behind cables claim that audio and DMX cables are made differently, with different impedances and intended uses. I used to belong to the first group; I used microphone cable and did not notice issues. If you own 2 or 3 lights, you might discover the same thing. However, I too came to side with those that advocate the use of proper DMX cable. After all, it is specifically made to carry a DMX signal and does this job flawlessly.

Do yourself a favor, and instead of trying to save a dollar or two by buying the wrong cable, buy proper DMX cabling and relish the absence of stress that may be caused if your lighting show malfunctions at an event. When purchasing DMX cable, you will probably want a few 5-foot or smaller lengths to go in between your lights, and a 20 or 25-foot length to go from your DJ booth up to the first light.

Lastly, I have to add a few words on the importance of a **DMX terminator**. A terminator is inserted into the last light in a chain and serves to stop the flow of DMX signal, preventing random actions by the lights in your chain. This was also something I neglected to use for a while, but after purchasing one (for a mere $6 I might add) I wouldn't switch back to not using one for anything. As your light show grows, a terminator will be essential to prevent lights from behaving erratically.

3 Pin and 5 Pin DMX Terminators

Programming Your First Light Show

Now, I'm going to give you an example of some simple programming that you can do to get your toes wet with DMX. For our imaginary light show, we will have the following lights:

- 4 LED RGB Wash Lights
- 2 Moonflower Lights
- 2 Scanners

We are also going to imagine we have a simple I-Beam trussing system. We will arrange our imaginary light show from left to right in this order: wash light, scanner, wash light, moonflower, moonflower, wash light, scanner, wash light. We will plug in our long DMX cable to the output of our DMX controller, and to the input of the first light in our chain. Remember, cable management! Make that DMX cable look pretty as it goes up the side of your truss! Next, we will connect a small DMX cable to the output of the first wash light, into the input of the scanner. Then, from the DMX output of the scanner to the next wash light, and so on down the chain to our last light. Lastly, we will plug a terminator into the output of the last wash light to finish off the chain. We will go back to the first wash light, and on the LED menu on the back of the light we will navigate to the DMX section and set the address to 001. We will set *all of our wash lights* to the same address (001) so that they will all react the same as we program. The next step will depend on whether you have a hardware DMX controller or a software version. I will put the instructions for both.

Hardware: Most hardware controllers have a set number of channels you can control on each fixture. For example, some controllers can control 16 lights with 32 channels each. Others can control 8 fixtures with 10 channels each. You will have to check your controller's manual to figure out how many fixtures and channels you can control. Let's say your controller does 16 fixtures with 32 channels each. We would set our first wash light to 001. Even though this light may only use 4 channels (red, green, blue, and dimmer), the controller has set aside 32 channels just in case. That means the next fixture in your chain (the moonflower in our example) would be set to channel 33, regardless of how many channels your first light uses. The next light in the chain (the scanners) would be set to channel 65. This is one of the limits of a hardware controller; you are restricted to how many fixtures your particular controller can handle. However, many beginner DJs will not be using more than 16 separate fixtures anyway, so this should not be too big of an issue. Heck, I only use about 4 maybe 5 different effects in most of my shows anyway. But, if you wanted to program each of your 4 wash lights to separate colors instead of them all acting identically, this would take up 4 more fixture slots. You can see how slots can fill up fast in that way.

Software: Once again, those with software controllers have it easy. In a lighting program, all you have to do is search for a fixture's "profile." A profile is a pre-programmed file that some poor designer already made for you that contains all the information about how many channels a certain light has and what they do. All you do is search by brand, find your light, and insert it into the program. That's it! Most software programs are not as limited as a hardware controller because they don't have to set aside *(x) number* of channels for each light. If you program a light that has 4 channels to channel 001, it will use the first 4 channels of your program. Now, you can look up your next fixture and insert it right behind the first on channel 005, without wasting tons of channels for a simple light! In this way, you can fit many more fixtures into your program than you could with a hardware controller. After you have inserted all of your fixtures into your program, just go to each light in your chain and set its address to correspond with the addresses you assigned in the program. After you have set all of your lights to the correct addresses and turned on your controller, you are ready to program. As far as the specifics of how you enter "programming mode" on your individual controller and record scenes, I unfortunately cannot cover every situation in this book. There are so many controllers on the market it would take too long to walk you through every model. Just know that you must take your controller out of "blackout" mode and make sure you enter "programming mode" (usually by holding down a button marked program). After setting your lights how you want them to look with the faders, you will press a button that says something along the lines of "record" and then push a numbered scene button to record those positions to that scene. Once again, consult your controller's manual and YouTube videos to become familiar with your specific controller.

TIP: If you're programming on a hardware controller, keep the manuals to your lights handy because you will need to consult them to know which channel will control which attribute of your light. If you are programming on a software program, each channel is usually labeled within the software.

So now that we have our imaginary light show rigged up, cabled together, and ready to program, let me walk you through how I would normally program a simple light show. First, I would have my manuals for each light close by (see tip above) so I can see what each fader will control. I would start with my wash lighting, selecting fixture one (or whatever I programmed them to). I would bring up the main dimmer to full on, and then bring up the red fader so that my wash lights were on full red. **Next, I would deselect fixture 1, so that any subsequent movements with the faders I make next won't mess with the red I just set.** I would select fixture 2, my scanners. I would bring their dimmer up, and then move the fader controlling the color wheel until they are red as well. I might move the pan and tilt faders to aim my scanners at the dance floor or ceiling. **I would deselect fixture 2** and move on to fixture 3, the moonflowers. To shake things up, I would bring up their dimmer and then the blue fader to add a second color to my scene. I could also bring up the fader that controls rotation and add a slow rotation to get some movement in my scene. Most moonflowers also have a channel that controls speed, so I could use that fader to make the rotation faster or slower. After deselecting fixture 3, I can hit record and *SCENE 1* to save the scene. Congrats! We have our first scene, a red and blue scene with a little bit of movement.

I'll usually program a few simple scenes like this with slow movements that I can use for song breakdowns and slow dances. There is nothing more annoying than slow dancing with "rave lighting" going on, so by having some slow scenes I can create an atmosphere conducive to the song (which is the whole point of lighting control anyway). I also program some scenes with medium-fast movements, which are great for hip-hop songs and other songs around 80-110 BPM. Finally, I record faster scenes to use for dance music, EDM, faster pop, and anytime I want to amp the energy up. Normally, I use cooler colors (blue, purple, pink) for slow scenes and warmer colors (yellow, red, white) for fast scenes. Some scenes are one solid color, others have 2, and rarely some have 3.

One of the best ways to program your lights quickly is by using the light's built-in **macros.** Macros are color chases, dimmer fades, and movements that were pre-programmed by the lighting manufacturer at the factory. Usually, they are kept on one of the channels in the light and can be accessed by bringing up the dimmer and then the **macro channel fader.** Now, instead of you programming multiple scenes to create color chases or complex movements, you can simply use the built-in macro effects and take advantage of someone else's programming. Experiment with your lights and see what macros are available. Select a fixture, bring up its dimmer, and very slowly slide the channel fader up that corresponds to the light's macros to cycle through the different programs.

TIP: The macros available on the macro channel are usually just the auto programs available when the light isn't being used with DMX. If you have been using a light without DMX control and love a particular auto program in the light, you can access it through the macro channel.

Once you have created a few scenes, you can exit programming mode and enter "live" mode. Now, when you push the scene buttons your recorded to earlier, you can recall those same lighting settings in time with the music and take your event to the next level.

Triggering Your Scenes

If you are programming with lighting software, it is completely possible to use your mouse to click the individual scenes you have created. In a live situation, this process can be slow and tedious. Luckily, almost all lighting programs have a way to trigger your lighting using your computer's keyboard or a midi device. Now, instead of clicking each scene separately, you are able to simply press a key on your keyboard and your scene will be triggered. The process for assigning scenes to keys is straightforward but will vary slightly depending on which company's software you are using. Generally, a right click on a scene will bring up a small menu. One of your options should be "button trigger" or something of that nature. Follow the prompts to select a key that will trigger that scene. You might notice the option to program midi commands to call up scenes. While this is a slightly more advanced method of programming, the process is similar. Simply connect a midi-mappable device to your computer and start your lighting program. Access the "button trigger" menu once more and select the midi option. Clicking the **learn** button will tell your computer that the next button you press on your midi controller is meant to control that scene. Pick a button, press it, and now that scene is assigned to that button. Midi controllers often offer more buttons for programming that are tactile and more responsive than a computer keyboard, allowing for quicker and more accurate scene changes.

I know that this chapter was probably not near as long as you had hoped it would be, but it should help get you on your feet and not be as mystified by DMX as you were before. Honestly, your light manuals and your controller manual will be your best friend through this process, and there are a plethora of tutorial videos online to help you master the process.

TIP: As I mentioned at the beginning of this chapter, I have written a 2nd book (available on Amazon) that deals wholly with DMX. If you find yourself struggling with DMX or just want to have an easy-to-understand guide as you learn it, I suggest you check out that book after you finish this one!

Chapter 7 – Getting Creative

Unique ways to set up and use lighting

A lot of what I will include in this chapter I have learned from the great Brian S. Redd of YouTube fame as well as the other dozens of other mobile DJs whose videos I've watched. This chapter is dedicated to offering examples, suggestions, tips, and tricks on how to set up your lighting in unique ways. It's not necessary that you get extremely creative at every event you do. For many events, your light show could be as simple as throwing all of your lights on to your lighting stand of choice and aiming them at the dancefloor. After a while, however, this gets monotonous and boring. If you do many of your events from referrals and word of mouth, people will notice you using the same setup for all of your gigs. By varying the placement and use of your light fixtures, you can deliver a fresh presentation to your clients and be known as an innovative and interesting mobile DJ. Feel free to come up with your own unique setups and post pictures of them in the review section of this book; I would love to see them!

Variations on the standard "lights on a T-bar"

So for a long time now, you have been simply rigging your lights to a T-bar or two and turning them on. Sure, it's worked for a while, but it's time to shake it up. Have you tried mounting some lights beneath the bar and some lights above the bar? If you're using 2 T-bars, have you tried mounting an LED bar vertically down the center posts? Do you usually position your wash lighting on the outer ends of your bar? What if you moved them to the middle and crossed their beams onto the dancefloor or ceiling? You could create some depth by moving 2 lights off of your T-bar and onto your speaker stand poles. Sometimes, less lighting on your T-bar looks better than stuffing it full of lighting. As always, remember to keep thing symmetrical! Nothing makes a T-bar look worse than 4 different lighting fixtures that don't match.

Lighting your dancefloor from other locations

It's not always the best idea to wash your dancefloor directly from your lighting stand or speaker stands. Especially with low ceilings, you will create a "truck headlights" feeling when you aim your wash lights straight at the dancefloor, blinding the guests the whole night. If you're in a smaller room, opt instead for placing your lights against the wall behind you aiming up, bouncing the light off onto your dancefloor. You can also buy a white tablecloth or scrim and put a wash light or two underneath, creating a focal point and washing your dancefloor at the same time. The same goes for speaker scrims; if you use them, place an LED par or bar behind them to add additional color and light to your dancefloor. Obviously, if you are doing uplighting around the room you can get a great dancefloor wash without having to light the dancefloor specifically. If you do decide to leave your wash lighting on the stand (which is often necessary), aim your lighting **over** the heads of your crowd to the back wall, or onto the ceiling. With low ceilings, bouncing light in this manner helps guests to avoid going blind and is more enjoyable overall.

TIP: Too often we DJs are confined to a corner of the room or dancefloor with no space directly behind us to put a lighting stand. No worries! If you're stationed on one corner of the dancefloor, see if you can place your lighting T-bar or stand on the opposite or adjacent corner. Look for a location that <u>won't</u> be an eyesore or overly distracting, and make sure to step back after setting up to see if things look professional.

Using multiple areas of the room

One of the easiest ways to increase the impact of your light show is to spread it throughout the room. Obviously, this method will only work if your space is big enough. If you are using 2 lighting stands, placing one in each corner of the room or on each corner of your dancefloor will help to spread the light out and make your light show seem bigger. Also, moving one of your lighting stands to the other side of your dancefloor or room can also spread the light and create the impression of size. What's most important when using this method is remember to hide your cables and tape them down well with gaff tape. If spreading your light show creates a mess of cables, the negative effects are greater than the positive ones. Another way to use multiple areas of the room is by aiming lights at the far corners, at specific spots on the ceiling, at interesting room details such as columns or pillars, or at each corner of your dancefloor.

Using a stage

If you are lucky enough to be placed on a stage or a riser, this is a great opportunity to add depth to your light show. Normally I am against placing lighting on the floor, but an elevated stage is a different story. I have often placed moving heads onto the edge of the stage (safely secured, I might add) to add another dimension to my lighting. Instead of all of my beams of light coming straight down from the truss, I now have beams crossing upwards. You'll see this strategy used often on tour by artists, so watch for it at the next concert you attend. I would advise you to never place your wash lighting on the stage, however, as this is usually close to eye level or slightly below the eye level of the guests. Setting wash lights on the stage like this will blind the first row of guests and cause the lighting to be blocked by bodies.

Using IR remotes

IR (infrared) remotes are coming free with more and more lighting fixtures these days. These handing little remotes are small, light, and easy to use. Instead of having to haul a DMX controller to every event and program your lighting, an IR remote can allow you to have some basic control over the functionality of your lighting without having to run DMX cable between fixtures. These remotes can control functions such as blackout, auto or sound mode, color, program, strobe, or dimmer. Often for small weddings or parties, I will just take the IR remotes for my fixtures and turn different fixtures on at different points of the night, creating variety easily. IR remotes are also very useful when it comes to uplights; instead of having to program each individual light on its own LED screen, you can simply walk up, point the remote, and choose a color! It makes setting your lights a breeze and saves you valuable setup time. I would say that if you are not using DMX but have IR remotes, always bring them to your events. Don't leave all your lights on and make it feel like a circus; use the remotes and create some surprises and action.

Chapter 8 – Wedding Lighting

One of the best upsells for your business

When I first started out DJing, I did not want to be a wedding DJ. I had done one or two and decided they weren't really for me. Sure, the money was great, but all of that prep, extra effort to make everything look perfect, the pressure of messing up a first dance or ceremony, etc.; It downright did not interest me! Then I slowly became an adult and realized that while the club and college parties were fun, in my market they paid nothing compared to a wedding. When you have a gear addiction like I do, you have to find a way to pay for that gear or you're up a creek. So, about a year ago, I realized that weddings were actually not as bad as I thought originally. Is there more prep time involved? Yep. But is the end result that much more satisfying and worth it? I would say so! But this chapter isn't about my conversion to being a wedding DJ, it's about the other part of my business that grew exponentially as I did more and more weddings. And that, my friends, is lighting.

Lighting at a wedding is usually different from my other events. Sure, every once in a while you have that bride that wants her wedding to feel like a club and asks for every piece of intelligent lighting you have. Mainly, however, lighting for weddings consists of subtler, calmer, and more elegant selections. At a wedding, lighting is used to create highlights, focal points, and ambiance. It's about making decorations and centerpieces stand out, and drawing attention to the most important people in attendance; the bride and groom. Wedding lighting is where your creative side can come out, and together with your bride and groom, you can create some amazing art with lighting. In this final chapter, I want to go over some of the most popular wedding lighting options and how they can dramatically boost your company's revenue.

Uplighting

When people think of wedding lighting, this is what they think of. In my opinion, uplighting can change the feeling of a room more than any other type of lighting or decoration. It allows you to dim the harsh overhead fluorescent lighting and envelope the space in the couple's wedding colors. An uplight is simply an LED par or bar that is positioned on the floor, against the wall, pointing up. This creates a column of light that stretches toward the ceiling. By positioning your lights at intervals along the walls, at the base of columns or pillars, or below other important architectural elements, you can highlight and draw attention to different areas of the room.

Often, uplighting is used along the wall behind the head table, drawing guest's attention to the bride and groom. Uplights are usually sold to the client in sets of 4, 8, 16, etc.… (you get the idea). Depending on the demand in your market, as well as your ability to sell them, different types of lights may work better than others for you. Right now, the hot item across the country is the battery powered uplight. These rechargeable pars eliminate wires and some of the hassle of setting them up. The added portability comes at a cost, and it's up to you to weigh that cost versus the benefits. Personally, I only own a few battery pars. This is because, at the large majority of the weddings I do, there is plenty of power to spare, and saving a lot of money per light is worth the extra few minutes of cable management to me.

TIP: Since publishing the first edition of this book, prices on battery-powered uplights have continued to drop. Good news for DJs! Getting into the battery-powered uplight game is easier and cheaper than ever, and now might be the time for me to eat my original words and say that ease of use for a battery-powered uplight is definitely worth spending a little more.

Color choice is also important when selecting your uplight. Up until the last few years, almost all uplights were simple RGB units. While you can create thousands of colors with only red, green, and blue diodes, the addition of amber, white, and ultraviolet diodes broaden the spectrum that is available to you. If you find yourself getting a lot of requests for uplighting, investing in quad (RGBA, RGBW, or RGBUV), or hex (RGBWAUV) colored uplighting may be a good option. Again, the added versatility comes at an added price.

An important aspect of uplighting is how you integrate it into the rest of your light show. I am from the school of thought that uplighting is meant to add atmosphere and mood to a room, not be the main light show when dancing starts. Often, I see uplights that suddenly become flashing multi-colored strobes that are more disorienting than tasteful. I prefer to set my uplights to the color(s) my bride selects, and leave them like that for the rest of the night. I leave the architectural lighting on the architecture and the dance floor lighting on the dancefloor. Think about it; if your whole room is suddenly full of lighting action, do people have any incentive to move to the dancefloor? Additionally, if grandma is trying to relax towards the back of the room, sending her into an epileptic seizure definitely isn't a good thing. Dance lighting can be overwhelming to some, and these people need a space where they can go and relax their eyes while observing the dancefloor from a distance. I'm sure many of you disagree on this point, and that's ok! There are always "what if" situations, and if you have the right bride and groom and the reception calls for it, go ahead and program those uplights.

Cakespotting/Pin Spots

A pin spot is a small, concentrated spotlight that used to be commonly used to illuminate mirror balls. In the wedding lighting industry, a pin spot is often used to highlight the cake, centerpieces, or other important details. Traditional pin spots contained actual bulbs and had attached cords that severely limited their portability. Thanks to today's battery technology, pin spots are more portable and easy to use. Chauvet sells a pack of 6 with a special case that charges all of them simultaneously for less than $200. American DJ also sells similar lights. These pin spots come with brackets for attaching to drop ceilings, as well as powerful magnets for attaching to anything metal. Pin spots can easily be hidden out of sight on the ceiling or above eye level. Using pin spots to spotlight a cake, card table, sign in book, or other details is one way to draw attention to the most important details of the reception.

Monograms/Gobos

You probably are already familiar with what a gobo is from our earlier discussion of moving heads. To recap, a gobo is a metal or glass stencil within a light that shapes the light into a certain shape. The great thing about gobos is they can be made into almost any design imaginable, including text or logos. This is where gobos apply to weddings. Commonly called **monograms**, these custom gobos can be designed with a couple's initials, names, wedding date, and pretty much anything else you can design in Photoshop. Whether they are simple steel or the more complex (and expensive) glass variety, there are many online suppliers that have online ordering forms and design programs. But a gobo alone will not make a monogram; you need a gobo projector. While you could technically insert a custom gobo into a higher end moving head that allows for interchangeable gobos, this could be a cumbersome process. Luckily, there are lighting fixtures specifically designed for the purpose of projecting gobos. They come in all shapes and sizes, from large projectors that utilize lamps down to compact battery-operated fixtures.

Both American DJ and Chauvet make a compact, white, battery-operated gobo projector that can be mounted practically anywhere and is surprisingly bright for its size. These smaller gobo projectors are a great option for the mobile DJ, due to their portability and ease of use. The slot that holds the gobos easily slides out and you can change gobos in a matter of seconds. They have IR remotes that allow them to be mounted out of sight and controlled without standing on a ladder and flicking a switch.

Custom monograms have a great ROI; once you have the projector paid off, depending on the type of gobos you order (or make), you can make $100-$300 per gobo. One final note: your clients don't always need to order custom gobos. Many projectors come with stock images that are marriage-themed, and you can sell these stock gobos to your brides for a reduced price. Another common strategy is to have a custom monogram flanked by other designs that are designed to fill space on the wall. These "breakup" patterns do exactly that; break up the normally boring and blank wall space with an intricate and elegant pattern.

Ceiling/Tent Washing

One of my favorite lighting services is ceiling washing. Using bright LED wash lights with wide beam angles (my favorite is the Chauvet WashFX), you can literally flood the ceiling with color and further dim the harsh overhead lighting. There is nothing like walking into a ballroom that is glowing with the couple's wedding colors. Ceiling washing is a relatively easy process, and the most difficult part is finding a place to mount your lights where they won't aim into the eyes of the guests. One thing that is essential when looking for fixtures to do a ceiling wash is the ability to color mix within the fixture itself. When you're trying to dial in an exact hue for your bride, being able to adjust the red, green, and blue values right there on the back of the fixture makes the process SO much easier. Use ceiling washing carefully, and only with colors that lend themselves to quality pictures (or you'll have an angry photographer on your tail). Amber is a very popular color, along with soft pinks and purples, and warm white.

TIP: Green is usually never a good choice for spotlighting a couple or washing a room. It makes people look sickly, something photographers (or anyone really) aren't fond of.

Uplighted Tables

Another great use for your uplighting lies underneath the tables at the reception. If your bride and groom opt for white linens, placing a par or bar under a table aiming upward can make the table glow in an awesome way. Lighting the head table is often the easiest option, as you can use either corded or battery-powered uplights. If your bride and groom want lighting underneath each table for dinner, uplights with a battery are by far the easier method.

Chapter 9 – Conclusion

My final 2 cents and a few more thoughts

I hope that as you have read this book, you have learned something new. Whether buying this book was your first step in venturing out into mobile DJ lighting or simply a quick read to see someone else's perspective, I hope you can take something from its chapters and apply it to your own business. The greatest part of this book is that many of these suggestions and tips can be applied right now, with the lights you already own. If you are looking to branch out and expand your arsenal, hopefully you have gotten some ideas as to which fixtures will bring you the greatest returns and be the most versatile for your business model.

Just like mixing, lighting design can take practice. Network with local venues and offer to set up your lighting and take pictures that the venue can use to show potential clients. Many venue owners are eager for free promotional material, and as a bonus, you get to experiment with different rooms and setups. If you don't feel like packing your gear up, set up different lighting systems in your living room or backyard. It's a lot more fun to be creative when you don't have 1 hour to set up before your wedding starts. Before the day of an event, look at pictures of the venue online if you haven't been there in person to help brainstorm lighting ideas. Email the venue manager and ask for a floor plan (which is a great idea for any mobile DJ, by the way). In short, make sure that you have at least come up with a rough idea of what you plan to do with your lighting before the day of your event.

Never stop learning. I have practiced and practiced and used lighting weekly for the past few years, but I still find myself reading books, watching videos, and constantly striving to learn more about lighting. If the science behind lighting fascinates you, learn what you can about that! If the events put on by other lighting technicians are an inspiration to you (they are to me), watch their videos. I don't think I can go to a concert anymore without constantly analyzing the number of moving heads, the placement of the truss, and the color combinations used. I am always looking for ideas and inspiration that I can carry over to my events.

When it comes to lighting, sometimes it's fun to just buy a light for yourself. I know many DJs who got into this business simply because they loved to buy the gear. Heck, I don't think I *really* have a *need* for multiple lasers, but man they sure are fun. I spend a lot of time watching the promo videos put out by the different lighting manufacturers and dreaming of lights I wish I had. Sometimes, I'll buy one just because I want to have something no one else has. Some people spend their money on their car or their closet; me, I buy lights. My point; if this becomes a passion to you like it is for me, treat yourself to a fun effect light, laser, or other special light every once in a while. There is a certain giddiness that comes when you open a package with a new light in it.

If you have enjoyed this book, I would **love** a review on Amazon. Reviews help others find and use this book as well. If you have suggestions or comments, please add them to your review. This book will likely undergo revisions as the industry changes even more, and knowing what readers want to learn will help me make these updates.

Thanks for reading! I wish you best of luck in your mobile DJ lighting quest!

Printed in Great Britain
by Amazon